Copyright © 2022 Tekkan
Artwork Copyright © 2022

All rights reserved.
First Printing, 2022
ISBN 978-1-7363537-7-6

To contact Tekkan please email:
buddhaboy1289@gmail.com

Table of Contents

Monkey Mind. . . . . Page 92

How to Read My Poems

I want to be direct in my meaning — I want people to clearly understand my meaning. My wordiness is inspired by Shakespeare, and the (aimed-for) concision is in imitation of Japanese style. Using the sonnet with the tanka, I mix the sensibility of the Occident and the Orient — which I have done by living in England, Japan, and America.

I have married the sonnet to the tanka. I tell a story in the sonnet. The story builds to a conclusion in the last line. The tanka is a commentary, or a counterpoint, to the sonnet — the combined poems have two endings.

Recently I have added limericks and doggerel into my repertoire. The limericks have a rhyme scheme but the tanka do not.

I don't punctuate much in my poetry. I want the words themselves to do the work. There is logic between words, and the forms provide structure. By not using punctuation I hope to direct readers to carefully attend to each word — to appreciate the graininess of words.

Reading my poems silently and reading them aloud may be different experiences. There's not always a pause intended at the end of the line.

Hint: *sonnets are to be recited not as lines but as phrases, and a phrase often overflows the break at the end of a line. I pause and take a breath where it seems natural for me to pause. Another person may pause differently than I do.*

Each poem is a piece of a mosaic, and it is my hope that the collection of poems forms a portrait of consciousness.

My friend, *Will Ersland*, is a wonderful artist. His artwork graces this book.

I am Barry MacDonald. I received the *dharma* name *Tekkan*, which means "Iron Man," a settled practitioner of great determination.

— *Tekkan*

Everyday Mind XXV

Like all the trees
this maple is bare again —
the sky is white.

The truck's engine is roaring up the hill
Filling the morning air with commotion
A consequence of its locomotion
And I appreciate it with good will
Admitting that it's giving me a thrill
Thinking about the driver's devotion
The selfless service of his emotion
His destination being the landfill
As the truck is serving society
By picking up and hauling away a
Week's accumulation of garbage
The effluvium of technology
As it is a necessary and a
Helpful ennobling kind of cartage.

Conversation with
the average garbage truck
driver would be
better than that of a
typical politician.

There is a bush still holding on to its
Leaves right next to Cub Foods where I hear a
Bevy of tiny birds engaged in a
Twittering fit that's not even a bit
Self-conscious as I approach and they get
Quiet as I stand — and then I go a
Little way away and wait — and then the
Racket starts again sounding like half-wit
Commentary — so once more I creep near
And quickly a silence ensues again
But soon there comes a sniping here and there
And I really do think the little dears
Are upset with me and are making it plain
They want privacy and don't want me here.

I think this is the
reincarnated spirit
of a gossip who's
been disembodied into
separated synapses.

I've been thinking about my dignity
Because it often is about the size
Of attendance and I want to apprise
Myself of the best time auspiciously
For me to kick the bucket skillfully
With consideration to maximize
My funeral and not to minimize
The recitation of the litany
Of my accomplishments and I'd like to
Be sure that the story of my travels
And of my publications is told and
I'd like people to have a clear-cut view
Of my selflessness and of the travails
Of my entire life that weren't bland.

Perhaps the crematory
Would be most laudatory
So fling my ashes
In ocean splashes
And be celebratory.

Of course there wouldn't be much benefit
To having a ceremony while not
Enjoying it so I've given some thought
To faking my death writing my obit
Hosting my funeral where I could sit
In disguise among the entire lot
Of my acquaintance to see how distraught
They were and I certainly do admit
That I'm being quite melodramatic
But I'm curious about what they would
Say about me and afterward I'd just
Remark that there was some kind of mistake
Or misunderstanding and then I could
Say the newspapers aren't worthy of trust.

It's not about vanity
Or about my sanity
I'm not bitter
I could live better —
Improve my humanity.

I like to capture the moments of change
In the seasons and the predominance
Of the bare branches — and the somnolence
Of the trees arriving again feels strange —
And the appearance of snow helps to gauge
The sudden shift before my consciousness
Adjusts — as it is the coincidence
Of my watchful and considerate age
That I notice when most of the trees are
Stark and the snow is coating the branches
For the first time this year — as I have seen
This sight under a white sky that is far
Above for decades and today it is
Clear the impact of the branches is keen.

Branches are so
weirdly
explosively
gesturing and yet
they are dormant.

I am like the barn owl gripping a branch
In the woods on the verge of the setting
Sun meditative freezing and hunkering
Down and I am summoning strength to stanch
My dreary thoughts that like an avalanche
Are oppressing and perpetuating
A sense of impending gloom including
A hint of doom — and as winter blanches
The color from the earth so does the cold
Stiffen and sober me reminding me
That there are seasons of difficulty
That I can bolster myself and be bold
And that poised relaxation is the key
To happiness amid austerity.

The barn owl grips a
branch in the gathering gloom
patiently waiting
in the circumference of the
forest for the time to pounce.

How often does it happen that as I'm
Typing poems looking out my window
Experimenting with snappy lingo
That a chickadee appears passing time
On the hedge outside looking like a mime
Of joy hopping and flitting even though
The air enveloping him is below
Zero and so he embodies a chime
With winter and one might even say that
He rhymes with the cold even though he is
The slightest of creatures composed only
Of bone sinew and muscle without fat
Epitomizing effervescent whiz
Gamboling with frolicsome energy.

If only I could
be as frolicsome and spry
as a chickadee
amid the gloom of winter
my thoughts would be whimsical.

Sooner or later I am going to stop
Because writing sonnets isn't easy
And I wouldn't say that I am lazy
But I do have to write my agitprop
As political hijinks are nonstop
The quality of my thoughts is hazy
I'm thinking in rhymes and that's just crazy
It is true that every rhyme is a prop
Which I hope really pops and doesn't flop
Which truthfully serves as a sop to my
Ego which plays and habitually
Mops my insecurity on the hop
With my lines of nonsense that do not lie
That may well approximate poetry.

I do need some scrutiny
Of my insecurity
Rhyming is crazy
And makes me lazy
I'd rather have sanity.

Relaxation is very important —
If I could do it when I needed to
There'd be little else that I'd have to do
As I wouldn't be pensive or mordant
All my afflictions would be impotent
Insecurity wouldn't stick like glue
And whatever comes I could see it through
I'd be decisive — not ambivalent —
I'd like to be wholehearted while letting
Go of results so I wouldn't worry
But I can't do that very well and so
Now I am wholeheartedly accepting
My unquenchable insecurity —
Trying to relax — so it doesn't grow.

I have to relax
with however much of my
insecurity
there is at the moment and
there's nothing else to do.

Did you ever make a hideous face
With friends as a child — just being funny?
Today is laughing and smiling easy?
We humans communicate face to face
We have ample ability to grace
Our friends with affectionate repartee
Swapping carefree facial hyperbole —
When quiet and attentive we can trace
Our subtle and unspoken emotions —
But in our workaday ways our faces
Are serious and absorbed in our chores
Cogitating on mundane commotion
As we focus on faraway places
And much too often we find ourselves bored.

Hollywood actors
simulate sincerity
with lip-trembling clues
with watery eyes
with verisimilitude.

A crocodile doesn't show emotion
A snake can slither but it doesn't smile
An ostrich can scamper for miles and miles
Inexpressive in its locomotion
There are countless beings in the ocean
And most don't bother to demonstrate bile
As they eat each other in mindless style
A dolphin can be joyous in motion
An octopus is capable of play
An elephant shows wisdom in its eyes
A dog can be a source of sympathy
My Kitcat is frolicsome every day
Some animals are smart — and they don't lie —
They do lovable reciprocity.

We humans are
dubiously gifted with
politicians who
can deceive and accuse
innocent people with ease.

A holy person is liable to
Befuddle a novice by presenting
An odd statement of a nagging puzzling
Nature which the novice is supposed to
Ponder wholeheartedly and to come to
Absorb lovingly each of the words taking
The surface meaning and meditating
Over a day with nothing else to do
And as the mind naturally leaps from
Thought to thought to thought the absurdity
Of the teacher's remark asserts itself —
The eccentricity of the words worms
Itself deeper with an uncertainty
Whether the meaning will resolve itself.

If you wear shoes
with rubber soles
the whole world will
be covered with
rubber.

I'm not certain that a single-pointed
Concentration is the object of the
Exercise and I do suspect that the
Guru would like his words to be sampled
Like the bouquet of a fine wine inhaled
And absorbed throughout the hours of a
Day without the distracting snares of the
Frenzied rush of business complicated
By pressing problems needing solutions
Maneuvering crazy-making pressures
Burdened with a need for accomplishment —
But the guru does create the suspicion
That all of his nonsensical measures
Are only producing befuddlement.

When a pickpocket
encounters a saint
his only concern
resides in the saint's
pockets.

I'm sorry — it is hard to focus right now
I will do my best but I'm distracted
My poetry is being impacted
I want to do two things at once somehow
And I can't do either well anyhow
My phone is busy and I'm affected
Which is a thing I haven't expected
It's a situation that I allow
As I'm sitting at my desk trying to
Write poetry while also texting with
Women on Match.com — so that I am
Looking at my phone expectantly to
Finagle my talents as a wordsmith
And my head resembles a traffic jam.

The pacing of texts
is different from woman
to woman and it's
tricky to fashion the best
angle of approach with each.

Kitcat and I have been housemates for a
While and we understand each other well
And I can say he primarily dwells
Upon satisfying his appetite with a
Customary schedule and at times in the
Day he climbs on top of a small step stool
In the kitchen endeavoring to tell
Me that he is anticipating a
Serving of delicious treats which I keep
In a bag on the kitchen counter and
Then he yowls to summon my attention
And I am indulgent — though I don't leap
To placate him — but I lollygag and
Saunter and bellow to create tension.

Usually three
times in a day we do
a lion taming
routine — but who is training
whom is problematical.

How can I put my face to its best use?
Do I practice gestures with a mirror?
Can I make my sincerity clearer?
Should cordial expression be profuse?
Would passionate exhibitions seduce?
Could humble self-abnegation endear?
How should my curiosity appear?
And does subtlety produce the most juice?
When I observe Hollywood performers do
Their renditions of situations
They don't overplay their faces because —
Of course — they're comely and they don't have to
Impose their feelings with declarations
When elegant subtlety earns applause.

Perhaps I'd be much
happier if I forget
what my face does
and if I attend to
whatever is happening.

The window in front of my desk looks east
And there are oak trees to the west across
The street and the oak leaves are being tossed
By a wind finally having been released
And the leaves are falling making a feast
Of dissipation and I feel a loss
And I'm thinking how I can put across
The sweetness of melancholy increased
By the pace of descending oak leaves in
The air and the many trees before my
Eyes are already bare and their branches
Are moving in the wind to underpin
A tactile sense of disappearance tied
To patient curiosity that lives.

Just a few wispy
clouds moving southward give the
sky a pace and
a direction at odds with the
blustery movement of trees.

Oh! What my round bootlaces did to me
I'd walk around and they would come untied
Which was a constant slighting of my pride
With a forced feeding of humility
An unwanted idiosyncrasy
When all I wanted to do was to stride
And there I was frustrated standing astride
Sloppy laces — oh what idiocy —
And I'd have to bend over again in
Public places and retie the laces
Which seemed such an act of futility
And I couldn't be walking about in
Winter blizzards taking angry paces
With my laces trailing me shamefully.

A friend advised that
I had only to take the
rabbit ears of my
usual knot and double
knot and since then I do.

Don't think about what happened yesterday
And don't worry much about tomorrow
Wouldn't you rather belittle sorrow
To free your energy and get away
There's no use in fabricating doomsday
Settle yourself — and become a flambeau
If you're despondent then learn the banjo
Even responsible adults can play
You can surf the waves of your emotions
And while resting you may linger and watch
Disturbance dissipating before you
As it's all vibrating ceaseless motion
And nothing has to matter very much —
You need not be a miserable stew.

If only I could
learn how to relax just
when I wanted or
needed to then I could be
a harmless peaceful hippie.

It's not the same piece of winter sky that
I'm seeing outside the window as I'm
Breathing oxygen produced just on time
For this moment now and it isn't that
I'm insensitive or asleep or that
I'm unappreciative that winter rhymes
Year after year and that the seasons chime
Day after day but it's elusive that
I'm looking at the same twisty bare trees
And the so familiar high overcast
Sky and it seems that I've been here before —
Weary — still not knowing how to appease
A dreary restlessness — and yet a vast
Impending liberation is in store.

Looking past the same
bare branches — I remember —
it's a different sky
today and liberation
could happen in a blink.

Isn't it hilarious that so much
Energy goes into persuading a
Person to love you and I think it's a
Possibility that there's overmuch
Love available but that it is such
An elusive thing depending on a
Spontaneous connection that is a
Gift and all I can do is be in touch
With what I think is happening — even
Though it's true that I don't know — and isn't
It curious to play the role of a
Lost and lonely soul who does believe in
Surprises and to be one who doesn't
Quit and who is ready to be gaga.

Wanting love can be
a kind of hunger and so
I try to be as
light as a feather waiting
patiently to give my gift.

The thing I have to wrap my head around
Is the thought *nobody cares* which is a
Slap to a person's confidence and a
Blow to the ego which becomes a wound
When life's troubles appear as a beat down
And it seems that I am up against a
Tide of difficulty and I need a
Power greater than myself to face down
An impending sense of isolation
Of meaningless emptiness that can so
Easily take over a person's thought —
I am grateful for my incarnation
And am strong enough to take many blows
As I practice watching my train of thought.

Then I suppose that
the emptiness from which
everybody comes
is an indestructible
and curious *no-body*.

There is satisfaction in doing things
That are practical and tangible that
Everyone can grasp ahold of and that
They can appreciate which also springs
From accumulated talents and brings
A level of commercial reward that
Pays for all the necessary things that
Fill a household and takes away the sting
Of having to work so hard and I am
Thinking of a mason who works with bricks
And stone who applies his patience and his
Strength — a worthy workman using his hands
As I am sure he has mastered many tricks
Of his trade of which he's truly a whiz.

For three hours I
assembled an essay but
accidentally
deleted it with one
stupid tap on a keyboard.

It's not solely caffeine in my coffee
That I use to my advantage — and I'm
Sure the caffeine helps — but I know the time
Of the day when I have felicity
And I am most awake and it's easy
Then to connect my thoughts with words that rhyme
And then my emotions and grammar chime
Just when I'm having the most clarity
Because for most of the day I do my
Business on my own without the chance to
Use my words while I believe that life is
Best with conversation and I scrape by
Alone — as well as I might — but I do
Want to see what communication does.

I leverage
rhythmic energy
to communicate
with you who are
an open white page.

It's easy to blame politicians for
The screwed-up state of our society
As they take on responsibility
By simulating a show of candor
Knowing as they do it's hard to keep score
Of distant laggardly bureaucracy
Which creates societal entropy
While we citizens expect so much more
From our public servants and we tend to
Choose the politicians who are smooth at
Telling lies while we neglect to admit
That we would like to profit from a slew
Of subsidized government programs that
Can't last forever — as there are limits.

Those who exercise
power profit from
power — everyone
else squabbles over
scraps.

Do you suppose that he was serious
When he wrote those dozens of besotted
Sonnets in iambic bebop trotted
About as if he were delirious
With love which would be deleterious
To balance to be so tightly knotted
In confusion and to be so clotted
With passion appearing imperious
In one poem and then melancholic
In the next and isn't it curious
That he doesn't portray his lover with
Defined clarity which is symbolic
Of a fantasy and injurious
To the health of such an addled wordsmith.

Shakespeare's sonnets
are like the skull of Yorick
that Hamlet dug up
from the dirt — who can gauge
the jester's sincerity?

You know these sonnets are a fabrication
They're written in the spirit of a game
They're phantasmagoria without shame
As I am giving vent to my fixations
Where I can practice painless flirtations
Whereas real emotions can be a drain
And I would much rather play with the flame
Of a curious elucidation
And you may see each poem as a wall
Of words fitted tightly together like
The stones of Machu Picchu without
Mortar — or perhaps like the overall
Effect of a prosaic concrete dike
That says to a sea of boredom — keep out!

On every page of
this book there is a wall of
words wherein each word
does righteous duty without
any superfluity.

What does the whiteness of a page mean to
You as you turn the pages with the tips of
Your fingers as white is a color of
Purity and of being unsoiled to
The touch of the eye being easy to
Overlook as the words get the best of
Your attention and as the focus of
Curiosity the words proclaim to
You what is worthy of notice — but don't
Discount the quiet presence of paper
Sliced and so precisely weighted for the
Fingertips of readers because you don't
Recognize truth without the paper
Which is invisible — like the word "the".

Feathery clouds and
a new-fallen snow have a
soothing quality
so easy to overlook
against the pepper of life.

You have a story to tell and maybe
Your happiness comes in conversation
In simple and unhindered discussion
As the weight of experience is freed
And communication dispenses seeds
Of peace as you may escape delusions
Of all your self-punishing conclusions
As another person could set you free
With a healing of intimacy that
Dispenses with the need for caution as
There are people who can't be trusted but
Some of us are compatible with what
Feels so much like a hole in you and is
The burning of emptiness in the gut.

In my youth I met
a derelict old drunk who
asked me to write his
life's story but I didn't
have the energy for it.

For most people the holiday season —
Including Thanksgiving — is a time for
The gathering of family and for
The sharing of experience upon
The hardships that we don't have to dwell on
The getting over of life-numbing chores
And we have the chance to open the doors
Of our hearts to each other again on
Christmas and New Year's Day but for some of
Us there's a paradox of convention
That societal expectation makes
The spontaneous act of showing love
A difficult role that's full of tension
Inspiring a taste of sour grapes.

I'm grateful for the
Grinch who steals Christmas
for the elucidation
of the stubbornness
of the suffering.

There are deserts to cross on the way to
Liberation with the aspiration
With the impatience of expectation
That with mighty efforts I can accrue
The wisdom beyond wisdom and I do
The prescribed remedies for deflation
And I don't shirk my share of frustrations
And I have the resolve to see it through
Encountering the aftermath of the
Dissolution of my family that
Left me with a household full of items
Belonging to an ex-wife a son a
Daughter of trivial little things that
Bite me — what am I going to do with them?

I'm not ready for
the inspiration
of the memories
involved with every
trivial item.

An elephant is a ponderous brute
With provocative and curious eyes
It may be an impish elf in disguise
And it possesses a dexterous snoot
Which is a delicately touching snout
It makes use of its trunk to tantalize
To touch and caress and to socialize
And having such a limb must be a hoot
The elephant lumbers upon the earth
Its legs are like tree trunks with big round feet
Every footfall thuds and reverberates
Each echoing impact comes from its girth
It parades about in tuneful rhythm
Pounding about in a procession of beats
With thumping plopping steps that resonate.

The elephant can
hear the whopping of distant
elephants with the
sensitivity of its
attentive listening feet.

What would I do with an elephant's snout?
Could I turn the pages and read a book?
Or slice an onion with a knife and cook?
And turn a doorknob to get in and out?
And use a steering wheel to drive about?
Could I enclose a tulip's stem and pluck
Would I sniff a Coca-Cola and suck?
I'd swing it about if I were a lout
And could my elephant's appurtenance
Be an instrument of intimacy
Delicate enough to undo buttons
To unfasten bras with a nonchalance
To fondle soft breasts with intricacy
To probe inside of a bellybutton?

I guess the question
would revolve about whether
an elephant's trunk
would appear an enchanting
appendage on Match.com.

Every being possesses dignity
And I'm thinking of the worthy giraffe
Now you may be tempted to scoff and laugh
And read these lines for cheap hilarity
Which only shows your own barbarity
I am writing on the giraffe's behalf
And it deserves a witty epigraph
As it is an intriguing panoply
Giraffes don't care about your opinion
Giraffes embody elongated grace
Giraffes demonstrate curious caution
Giraffes exert a peaceful dominion
A giraffe has a respectable face
A giraffe is levity in motion.

To watch a giraffe
gallop over distance is
to see a loping
and a swinging grace that makes
locomotion beautiful.

It is not the most remarkable thing
About a giraffe and it looks puny
And it does appear a little loony
And if it chooses the giraffe could fling
It left and then if so inclined could zing
It right and when the giraffe is gloomy
It droops and when the giraffe is sunny
It swings and we could even say it sings
With happiness but it has prosaic
Use as the giraffe is assailed by flies
That tickle and bite the poor giraffe's rump
And there it is available to flick
The pesky flies before they even try
To bite — so the giraffe is not a grump.

The giraffe's plumy
tail appears exceedingly
laughable until
one sees it flick flies over
most of the giraffe's body.

He showers when he gets home at night so
He's free in the morning to wake and get
Out the door and he doesn't shave and lets
A week's worth of stubble grow and he goes
To work composed and I really don't know
How he can move without coffee and yet
That is what he does and he doesn't fret
Very much in his work-a-day tempo
Because he's done all the aspects of the
Job being a surveyor measuring
Distances and establishing order
About himself plotting points upon a
Grid and there's an ease in calculating
Numbers with no messes to get over.

If only people
in his life were as easy
to finagle as
numbers he wouldn't have to
grow loving roots into God.

I am attached to my morning shower
There are chores that I do before it
When waking I am only a halfwit
The minutes go by and I gain power
My brain gets going and my thoughts flower
Kitcat's hungry so I give him tidbits
I watch him run about — he doesn't quit —
When I don't feed him he does get sour
I traipse about the house for half an hour
Replenishing Kitcat's water and food
Taking care of his basement litter box
I read yesterday's poems and scour
Them for mistakes — I like my solitude —
My home resembles a childhood sandbox.

By the time I
enter the shower and
savor warm water
enveloping me my thoughts
are popping like popcorn.

Do you suffer from an attachment to
Your face being ever mindful of your
Appearance thinking it is a fixture
Of who you are that sticks to you like glue?
You can't escape no matter what you do —
And you do your best to create allure
To be genuine — but you are unsure —
Is your face only something you look through?
Is it even possible to think of
Who you are besides what you look like and
Can you imagine how differently
You would live without the idea of
Your appearance as if it were a brand
Which compromises elasticity?

How many hours
could you get by without a
mirror to make the
readjustments that you know
are absolutely needed?

We gather in libraries to read our
Poetry to each other handing out
Our poems and then we dangle our snouts
Over the pages to fuss and scour
Our verses trying not to be sour
Aiming to be helpful and not to spout
Piffle but to summon our best to sprout
Our creativity and to flower
In whichever way we choose to express
Because we want to use our freedom to
Say anything that we are moved to say
But how can we do that without finesse?
And I tend to be blind to my miscues
And it takes scrutiny to make headway.

Writing poetry
is like launching into an
acrobatic leap
and a writers' group performs
the job of a safety net.

I know I'm asking for trouble when I
Start reading profiles again but either
I act doing my best to be eager
Or I admit that I am too damn shy
And it's true that I'm not a quitting guy
So the goal becomes to be a seeker
While being mindful of my demeanor
But often all I can do is to sigh
While looking at girls on a dating app
Because no matter what I do it's so
That most of them don't bother to reply —
Yes — I know that is better than a slap
But I have to practice not feeling low —
It seems that the rules of hunting apply.

The object is not
to collect a harem but
to find one woman
who matches me well enough
to be a cozy couple.

There is quizzical Debbie to ponder
And she is not the one who is confused
But what she is doing has me bemused
She is a beauty which I can't ignore
With a sense of humor that I adore
My interest in her is already fused
But she leaves me feeling a little bruised
I can't determine what she has in store
She replies intermittently leaving
Me to dangle in between messages
Encouraging me by giving me her
Phone number but it is confusing
When I rouse myself and call she teases
By not answering — what should I infer?

She's agreed to meet
at India Palace after
the holidays which
is almost a month away
and does keep me lingering.

Sundays are my sanctuary when I
Can leave my bed at my leisure
And devote myself to mindful pleasure
Not having a work schedule to go by
When the heft of my business applies
I get to explore internal treasure
To plumb awareness and take my measure
And I am happy with what I come by
As I plant my bottom in my chair and
Fish for ideas in the air with the
View of my window — and every
Day mind is the game that I take in hand
And I know most of you would say — huh? —
Writing poetry is my reverie.

I am blessed by the
discovery that I can
lighten my mood by
playing with words and it's
fine being solitary.

I can imagine what it would be like
Having a girlfriend and devoting time
Nurturing each other trying to chime
Our emotions — and would I have to strike
A precarious balance not to spike
My poetry jazzing time? When I rhyme?
Could I be a boyfriend only part-time?
And I do hope that we could think alike
And give each other some necessary
Freedom because I can't imagine how
I could write with someone tapping or stomping
A foot behind me quite impatiently
With a furrowed forehead and angry brows
Devouring glowering souring.

Because once I sit
my rump in my chair time goes
by and I lose track
until it's late afternoon
and I've blown my energy.

The presence of the winter cold again
Can be a pleasurable sensation
A dash of bracing invigoration
It is a dance up to the edge of pain
And to partake of the season is sane
Winter can bring a touch of elation
One might even say it's a flirtation
With danger and I'm not one to complain
Except that I'd rather not meet winter
In my living room when my furnace stops
Working and I shiver trying to sleep
In a frosty bed and my breath appears
As ghostly vapor and I have to drop
Everything to fix it — I can't be cheap.

A fan went out in
my furnace and it cost me
$500
to fix it but winter was
banished from my living room.

I pine for female companionship but
Through painful experience I know by
Now that it does me no good to deny
The subtle hesitations of my gut
And to allow myself easy shortcuts —
Women say what they want and I comply
I am straightforward and I do not lie
And I guess it takes patience to abut
Myself with just the right woman who would
Appreciate me for who I am and whom
I could understand well enough without
Our having to argue and so we could
Grace each other and so we could assume
Love — without having to figure it out.

In America
I am wandering about
looking for a piece
of a scattered puzzle that
abuts on me perfectly.

How often do you look at things about
You before you stop noticing them as I
Am thinking of a sign that almost cries
"*Turn Off the Coffee Pot!*" which loses clout
Over time and so it does come about
That we do forget and afterward sigh
Because we don't remember — though we try —
We are not negligent — we are not louts —
The sign is something we don't think about
So the coffee burns into a hard crust
And has to be soaked chipped and then scoured —
Burnt coffee is difficult to get out —
The people at the church have lost their trust
It's true I think they have somewhat soured.

I think it's not a
bad idea to have on
hand a supply
of the glass pots easy to
dispose of from time to time.

The snow is falling in a steady pace
It is falling amid the homes and trees
Barren branches are swaying in a breeze
It is the morning but there's not a trace
Of the sun — the light is dim in this place
I am typing carefully on the keys
At the window watching snow at my ease
And I think the season is full of grace
Even as the color is erased from
The earth and there is no demarcation
Between the descending snow and the sky
And the scene will be dark for months to come
As this is the time for hibernation —
December is opposite from July.

This white paper page
represents new-fallen snow
and the ordered rows
of black letters on the page
stand for the barren branches.

The sun isn't visible so often
During winter and yet by mid-morning
The landscape is lighted — trees are moving
In the wind and the blusters aren't softened
By a touch of warmth and days are often
Devoid of obvious cheer and feeling
More than a little forbidding blending
Together over time and not softened
By the lively variety of growth
And yet the sun isn't really absent
And sometimes it appears as a shiny
Spot and — yes — the sky and sun are both
White — but the sun is certainly present
And it will be bright eventually.

Even behind clouds
the sun is incandescent
radiating heat
in every direction and
lighting a chilly day.

The mechanism of a furnace lies
Outside the sphere of my understanding
And mine is especially frustrating
Involving a magnitude of surprise
That it burns fuel oil and most of the guys
Who fix furnaces are discouraging
And my situation is perplexing
As the bulk of the profession applies
Itself only to gas furnaces but
With the use of my determination
I found a couple companies who work
With oil and though there wasn't a shortcut
I did experience a redemption
By utilizing an expert's artwork.

Charles is a wealth of
genial information
and he replaced a
fan and tuned my furnace and
now it hums musically.

The utterances of crows convey a
Conspicuous thrust of intelligence
Expressed insistently with emphasis
And it's tricky to know how much of a
Range of meaning is involved or of the
Sort of feelings — maybe not gentleness
And perhaps there isn't much eloquence —
And whatever they're expressing there's a
Guttural ruthlessness that seems to be
In play that implies that there's a pecking
Order within a tribal dynamic
And when I see them gather in a tree
I can't help but wonder what they're saying
And whether I could be sympathetic.

To hear a single
crow caw on a cold morning
and be answered by
another in the same tree
is to hear a weird language.

They fly and land and hop spryly around
The carcass on the road and in turn they
Stab and bite and swallow bits of squirrel
Meat and grudgingly they take wing to get

Out of the way of a passing car and
On another day five or six of them
Range about the yard assaulting the air
With their raspy voices as they fly from

The cottonwood to the apple tree to
The maple and it is apparent that
There is something going on in the
Company of the crows as they talk to

Each other alive to their own concerns
Being indifferent to outsiders.

People choose to call
a group of crows a murder
as there is the sense
of an occupation
about their eerie presence.

If they are the same size two crows appear
Identical as they share the same shape
And mannerisms and yet to them there
Are differences and to hear their pitch

Of guttural language is to feel like
An outsider hearing foreign banter
As there is intelligence conveying
Purposes and urgency and there is

Something going on and there are roles to
Be executed driven by other
Than human prerogatives and spurred by
Stimuli peculiar to the world of

Crows composed of a cooperative
Domination of a territory.

To be under the
gaze of a society
of crows is to feel
the touch of detached and
wary curiosity.

The movements of clouds over the spinning
Earth exerts a subtle influence on
My moods as I go about my business —
I do make it a practice to watch the

Clouds and the sunshine — when the sky is cast
Over with a white or a grayish pall
I fall under a spell and time drags and
Days merge and the gloom perpetuates a

Sense of dreary endurance to be borne
Which is merely the creation of my
Mind no more substantial than the water
Vapor composing the moving ceiling

Of cumbersome clouds showing me just how
Omnipotent vapor and thoughts can be.

The suspicion of
being trapped within a place
of confinement and
of being bound by the cold
of winter months is subtle.

But once the clouds dissipate and the sky
Is open to the sunlight again the
Weight of my oppression lifts and a thrill
Of joy arises and a clarity

Of detail engulfs me and I can see
The emerging lines of a jet's contrails
Slowly spreading over the sky to be
Crossed by another pair of contrails and

When I absorb the foot of new-fallen
Snow I can rejoice with the crisp shadows
Of crooked trees upon the pristine white
And there are the sparkling crystals that are

Refracting rainbow points of sunlight that
Make me imagine a blanket of jewels.

The press of events
within human involvement
overwhelms the touch
of what the sky is doing
until one notices it.

The ordeal of moving the snow off of
My Mom's driveway would be trivial were
It not for the fact that the big blower
Won't start and I've had to resort to a

Puny electric thing that looks like a
Toy and I don't know why the prodigy
Inventers couldn't fashion plugs that stay
Connected but they didn't so I swore

And had to bend over tiredly to
Insert the prongs into the plug again
Being careful not stumble upon
The tangled length of cord trailing behind

Me as the silly and impotent maw
Took forever to do its simple work.

The thing threw snow half
the width of the driveway
which made a heap of
snow double the snowfall which
was a joy to deal with.

How can the mixing of the sky and earth
Be captured with words on paper other
Than in play as yesterday it seemed that
A cloud had settled in the neighborhood

And swallowed the white fence the homes the bare
Trees as the snow on the ground melted and
A mist painted the branches and twigs gray
And today the pale grass appears again

And fine grains of snow are curling in the
Air and coming from a sky without height
As there is no demarcation between
The sky and the snow but there is a glow

About the sky and the crooked branches
Amid the snow are swaying in blusters.

It is a scene of
fire earth water and air
mixed together as
93 million miles off
the sun keeps on combusting.

It has occurred to me that I haven't
Adequately expressed gratitude to
You for the years of attention you gave
To my emailed poems — you read every

One — and you wrote encouraging notes in
Reply faithfully every morning and
I get up early but you rise before
Me and reading my poetry must have

Been one of the first things you did for years
And the magnitude of such a heartfelt
Gift strikes me now that you've ceased reading them
Because I did I suppose finally

Exhaust you — which doesn't reflect on you
But on me — as you are ever loving.

By the way
you missed the
hundreds of
rhymed sonnets
I've written.

I am a traveler on the earth though
I don't often leave the neighborhood and
There are times when fear and isolation
Occupy my thoughts and gloom weighs
heavy

On me and I know that I know that such
Oppressions will pass but that doesn't make
The sad hours easier and then the mood
Shifts and the extent of distance appears

And I can see again with clarity
To far horizons and the local
Crows lose their spectral quality and when
I see a crow taking funny steps on

The frozen ground with its scrawny legs I
See a fellow being making its way.

I am human
like any other — riding
waves — being
someone doing something
thinking I'm going somewhere.

In a quest to buy a new snow blower
I went to Bayport Printing House to talk
To a mechanical genius I know
Who just happened to buy one last week at

Lowes where there are Ariens or Craftsman brands
To choose from and I went to Lowes and saw
The differences between price and size
And I asked whether they deliver to

Homes — and then I checked the machines on sale
At Menards and discovered the laggards
There deliver but they're too lazy to
Assemble the blower so they drop off

The blower in a weighty box leaving
The customer with an unpleasant chore.

My nuts and bolts
genius said that a
maintained blower
can be expected to last
fifteen to twenty years.

Whether I can do my chores without fuss
Is a challenge for my best effort — and
The mowing of the grass about my house
In summer is pleasant exercise now —

Though for several years facing the doubtful
Prospect that the blower would start at Mom's
House has made every impending snowstorm
An occasion of possible doom — but

The weight of living in Minnesota
Where snowplows are constantly scraping the
Streets and thrusting heaps of snow aside — where
The burden of clearing snow with an old

Machine is lifting from my shoulders — helps
To turn an ordeal into easeful joy.

Doing things well is
easier with the right tools
and the prospect of
having a new snow blower
helps me to laugh with winter.

I put the broken-down blower by the
Curb as two different guys advised and
When I returned this morning the two-stroke
High-pitched roaring squat and wide red little

Monster that for twenty years spewed snow was
Gone as someone driving by is betting
He can fix it or use parts of it and I'm
Grateful I didn't have to transport it

Or pay to have it removed and I don't
Know much about mechanics but I
Got clever at working around the quirks that
Signaled its slow disintegration as

Everything weakens and then falls apart
And I hope to outlast the next blower.

The screws that held its
plastic cover in place were
set aside and lost
winters ago when I swapped
spark plugs one sub-zero day.

We should have gratitude for nobody
Nobody is genuinely honest
Nobody is passionately sincere
Nobody is reliably helpful

If you want love nobody can help you
Intimacy is found with nobody
When you are lonely nobody is here
Nobody completely understands you

Nobody holds the planets in orbit
Nobody causes the sun's combustion
Nobody created all kinds of birds
At heart nobody is mysterious

When you need answers to questions you can't
Articulate — please — turn to nobody.

Beyond every
wavy spinning quark
is nobody.

With two sisters inside the bathroom the
Preteen girl was happy lying inside
Of the bathtub and she smiled and held a
Stuffed bear and I read the headline about

Tornadoes in Kentucky and glimpsed the
Photo and I didn't pause to think but
Later I watched a TV news report
And realized mere moments after that

Photo was snapped the house was torn to bits
And that girl was wrenched by the wind and hurled
A great distance and found dead — and from the
Cheerful innocence expressed in her face

One might guess that she believed that the rush
To the bathroom was no more than a game.

The report revealed
that girl suffered from a
diseased liver and
yet she was a being of
angelic visitation.

I believe in the love inside of me
Though I have not been very skillful in
Its expression as my love is suppressed
By cruel whispers of unworthiness that

Burden my thoughts and as I hunger for
Affirmation in the behavior and
The expressions of others toward me I
Guess that the vibes I emanate are an

Obstruction — but my predicament is
Balanced by patience and pluck and by a
Practice of gentleness with others who
Don't know of my occasional anguish

Which amounts to a self-imposed sense of
Unique and befuddled separation.

I think the fire of
my attention is burning
away the burden
of the propensities of
the negations of my thoughts.

I think my love finds fruitful expression
In the dogged persistence with which I
Gather with people who were drunks and with
People who love people who are drunks and

I do no more with them than to share the
Experience of being an ex-drunk
Who could be a voracious drunk again
If I stop the practice of spiritual

Jujitsu — we celebrate together
Our mutual vulnerability
And somehow in the exchange of our words
We find the strength and hope to live apart

From addiction — and most of what I do
In our meetings is to simply listen.

One finds in our groups
an honest expression of
the attitudes and
emotions that are burdened
and our humor is magic.

I see the Imperial Chinese designs
On the plastic placemats underneath the
Rice cooker inside a cupboard in the
Kitchen which prompts a pang of emotion

About the delicious meals my then-wife
Made over years when our kids were growing
And attending public schools in Stillwater
While I was busy being a husband a

Dad a printer an editor and the
Sorrow of the loss of those days is mixed
With sweetness as I know we did our best
And that the plastic placemats are symbols

Of how we lived — each of us comes away
With different patterns of memory.

These worthless things
are of no further use
and yet the thought
of throwing them out
is so painful.

Imagine the imperative imposed
By the growth of a horn positioned in
The center of your long snout between your
Eyes which you couldn't directly see

But could only feel the imposition
Of its weight yet from looking at others
In your own herd who had the thing you would
Easily assume that you had it too

And relative to other animals
You'd know you were a brute with a barrel
Chest and muscled legs that pound and thunder
The earth when you trot and your eyesight is

Poor while your sense of smell is good but you
Wouldn't be aware of those distinctions.

If you were a
rhinoceros
how much of you
would be determined
by your horn?

If I were a brute flexing my brawny
Legs in a trot plopping my flat feet on
The earth I would take pride in my weighty
Barbarity knowing nobody could

Knock me over and I would swing my head
Poised to charge and apply my heavy horn
To interlopers and I don't suppose
Much diligence would be directed to

The flicking of my tail which serves only
To cover a puckering backside but
I think my nostrils would be paramount
As I'd have a mighty appetite to

Satisfy and I would follow my nose
Sniffing for delicious edible plants.

Rolling in the mud
would be luxurious and
useful for adding
a layer of protection
against the biting of flies.

If you were mostly a humanoid but
Were born with a rhinoceros horn just
Above your eyes and you were heavy with
Thick muscled legs and two rhinoceros

Flat feet could you live harmoniously
Among people — apart from how they would
Behave toward you — do you suppose you'd be
Disposed to sudden bursts of temper and

Could you escape the preoccupation
Of being so different and could you
Cope with mirrors and would you be able
To savor a passion for symphony

Orchestras and gourmet recipes or
Would you adopt criminal tendencies?

Just having the
rhinoceros feet would
be enough to skew
your life — could you safely
partake of ballroom dancing?

Love gets mixed up in everyday business
As I'm doing the pattern of my life
Needing to do things on a schedule that
Takes my energy as there's often a

Problem like being behind a slow car
When I want to drive quickly — while my
Thoughts do return to a person who
I care about who I'm not able to

Meet as often as I'd like and I have the
Compulsivity of desire — with the
Doubt her adoration for me equals
Mine for her — which amounts to a yearning

That isn't satisfied — and I'm not sure
That this "so-called" love is durable love.

There is a thirsting
for something or someone that
is proportional
to denial of access —
which makes desire powerful.

I can turn my confusion to the way
I choose to do the patterns of my day
Including the gibberish I lavish
On Kitcat who thereafter excitedly

Gallops through the house — and to the pleasure
Of pedaling my stationary bike
While listening to Alan Watts my beatnik
Guru expostulating the *dharma* —

And to the fascination found in the
Subtle manifestations of snow and
The puzzling mentality of crows — and
The birth of a new day as seen from the

View of the valley at Pioneer Park
When the sun spangles the clouds with brilliance.

Love spills quietly
unappreciated and
unconsciously from
me as I merge myself in
the world and feel a kinship.

After I struggled starting the machine
When I failed to understand that a key
Needed to be inserted I got the
New snow "thrower" going and feel the strong

Torque of it — even at a slow setting —
And the handle grips keep me further at
A distance than I'm used to and I have
To muscle it roughly around corners

As it's bursting with power and wavers
From side to side — which I will control with
Practice — and the metal skids of it bounce
Over the broken-down pebbly parts of

The driveway — and the first pirouette with
An inch of fluffy snow goes well enough.

The machine is built
For moving heaps of snow and
leaves behind it a
fine layer of snow that will
Need scraping with a shovel.

When earplugs lessen stimuli beyond
The workings of my body I can hear
The beating of my heart and listen to
Its rapid and constant sound and I can

Also follow the inhalation of
My breath as it enters my nostrils and
Swells my chest and then the exhalation
Releases and relaxes my body

And I am never separate from these
Life-empowering rhythms and when the
Frenzy of thought captures the attention
Of my mind it's a comfort to know that

I always have the simplicity of
Obtaining peace — in my breath and heartbeats.

I have to quiet
myself and separate my
attention from the
lure of compulsivity
to follow breath and heartbeats.

This is the morning of the solstice when
The dance between the earth and sun changes
And the northern hemisphere obtains an
Increasing portion of sunlight each day

And the cyclical movement of the earth
Isn't obvious as it's happening
But the ebbing and flowing of life is
Never separate from its pattern as

Life consists of rhythms within rhythms
And the urgency of getting things done
In the human world has its rightful place
But it's helpful to know I don't have

To earn either my beating heart and breath
Or the solstices — as they are all gifts.

Clouds rain snow fog dew
springs rills creeks streams rivers
rapids river falls
are life-affirming patterns
of the sky earth and oceans.

This is an animal of glory and
Style displaying a train of feathers and
A royal crest on its head and it has
Crystals in its feathers that shimmer in

Sunlight with a stunning ensemble of
Iridescence of yellow and brown and black
And teal and most prominently of blue
And green and it does flourish and flaunt

And flounce and unfold its train of feathers
Like a Japanese fan swiftly spreading
And revealing a hypnotic array
Of jewel eyes appearing suddenly like

Some unearthly Hindu deity that
Casts a spell and astonishes one's soul.

The male peacock shakes
his iridescent feathers
with jewel eyes and
emits a vibration that
jangles the female's crest.

What do you make of the unearthly gloss
Of the peacock as it's not prideful nor
Vain and takes its business of foraging
For subsistence and its rituals of

Procreation in stride and it doesn't
Dwell on its superfluity and is
Not aware of the hypnotic spell it
Casts on people prompting fascination

As it becomes a symbol of regal
Beauty bespeaking vainglorious pomp
As an excess of sensuality
While we make a fetish of the finding

Of a single peacock feather as if
Its possession portended good fortune?

No craftsman sculptor
designer jeweler
painter or poet
could have conceived of
a peacock's feather.

Lily the calico cat was left by
Herself last night and when I arrive at
My desk she grumbles her meows with an
Insistence that isn't normal and as

I'm sitting and typing she's daintily
Stepping on the scattered sheets of paper
And pens and round stones and books that are strewn
On the desk in front of the window and

The footing is precarious but she
Manages gracefully though she bumps and
Just about upends a thermos of
Coffee before I catch it as she rubs

Herself under my nose and chin brushing
Against my growing beard making it itch.

Mom is visiting
her grandkids overnight on
Christmas day and
Lily has abandoned her
usual indifference.

Whatever it was that went bang billions
Of years ago when the temperature
Reached 1,000 trillion degrees Celsius
Nobody was here to see it and it

Did happen silently as sound depends
On an atmosphere to be transmitted
And there was no space and there was no time
Because space and time depend on bits of

Something to be strewn about within the
Reach of emptiness before they arise
And so the human mind can't conceive of
The void inside the Big Bang except to

Say that it happened nowhere consisted
Of nothing and that nobody did it.

What happened
is continuing
everywhere
simultaneously
now.

Hollywood directors don't do justice
To the eerie realities of the
Alien worlds that exist within our
Solar system on Saturn's largest moon

Titan which has an almost endless sea
Of icy ethane and methane under
An atmosphere of an unbreathable
Nitrogen gas and whatever landmass

There would be consists of floating islands
Of ice and ground covered in an ethane
Snow and the color palette would range from
White with tinges of blue to bluish white

Which would make for beautiful sunrises
But nobody lingers to paint the scene.

Words on paper
may vaguely sketch aspects
of the appearance
of Titan but words belong
to humanity on Earth.

I'm using the tool of meditation
To throw off identification with
My ego as a separate something
But the impetus of the discipline

Somehow gets in the way as it's tricky
To relax and to let liberation
Happen of itself — I am playing with
Words to clarify my opinions and

Emotions and intentions while I know
That words are intellectual catnip
Which help to direct me but of themselves
Words won't open the gate to *satori*

Which brings to mind the vermillion *Tori*
Gates that the Japanese make for their shrines.

A *Tori* gate is
the simplest structure of
two upright posts
two crossing beams — making an
entrance into the sacred.

I have come to love the use of words as
Nothing is more pleasurable than to
Craft a line that is clear and concise and
That's easily understood and spoken

And I like to contain my poetry
Within ten syllable lines as if the
Form were rigid while the nuances of
Meaning were liquid which I pour into

Any arbitrary vessel of my
Choosing as if the sonnet were made of
Crystal and the essence of the words were
Pure water free of the impurities

Of redundancy and opacity
With an illusion of the taste of no taste.

Of course a poet
can't keep a fiddling ego
out of the poem
which is why I strum tunes of
self-deprecating humor.

For those with eyes to see the landscape in
Winter is dominated by the wild
Gesticulation of the leafless trees
Conveyed over distance in the drab shades

Of grayish brown and if you would like to
Sample an undomesticated and
Undiluted portrayal of what cosmic
Energy looks like attend to the shapes

Of branches and twigs turning and twisting
In a concatenation of angles
Of bizarre directions as if the growth
Of trees were spontaneous explosions

Devoid of any sense of symmetry —
Except each tree is balanced by its roots.

Yet there are
oaks maple apple
magnolia and pine
and each kind is
distinctive.

Matsuo Basho was a Japanese poet
Who could capture the whole cosmos in a
Bowl the Japanese use for drinking tea
Because he could listen and watch without

Any obstruction of thought getting in
The way so when he saw an old pond and
A frog and he watched the frog jump in the
Pond the plop of the sound of the water

Reverberates as clearly today through
The centuries — when he heard the blusters
Of the rain spattering the banana
Leaf beside his hut we too can hear the

Beginning of the rain as it blows in the
Wind and drops upon the resonate leaf.

The sounds of a frog
and water and wind
and rain and of a
banana leaf need
no translation.

Whatever did go bang billions of years
Ago began motion and the pages
That you are turning came from a tree that
Gained life from minerals in the soil and

From sunshine in the air — which cannot be
Separated from the thing that went bang —
The words on the pages communicate
Thoughts and thoughts do share the same source as the

Parrots in South American jungles —
Oceans and mountains — ethane and methane
Seas on Titan — unknown phenomena
On some 1,000 trillion galaxies —

Underlying phenomena is the
Unborn and undying liberation.

Thoughts arise
from quiet interludes
of simplest observation
pregnant with life.

With both of the dates that I've finagled
Inside of a month each needed to be
Rescheduled a day before and one was
Rejiggered several times — and I am

Elated to adjust and to swallow
Disappointment with grace as behaving
Otherwise is futile — though I wish things
Were easier — the first woman is a

Writer and ex-drunk like me so we share
A common lingo but sadly there was
No spark — but the other has a saucy
Ukrainian accent and she is a

Beauty and she is a meditator —
But she is also somewhat tentative.

I don't know whether
her standoffishness
is native to her
personality or is
a boundary to be crossed.

I've gotten over my self-consciousness
On first dates and I can present myself
Easefully spontaneously with words
And depending on her I am able

To be funny or to leverage my
Unusual enthusiasms my
Foreign travels my curiosity
But the introduction is a balancing

Act and I'm meeting a unique person
As she is a different droplet of
The same cosmos offering a new
Reflection of what there is and I would

Like to know whether we are similar
Harmonious and complimentary.

I have no clue what's
going to happen
and I look forward
to meeting the right
woman.

What is the pith inside of loneliness?
Does it come only from an absence of
Female companionship? Is it about
A disconnection from the status games

And the political slant that people
Impose? Can I lay the blame off on my
Parents for the things they did and didn't
Do? Does alcoholism have any

Weight after I've been sober for decades?
I need a particular type of touch
And hunger for facial expressions
I want the caress of another's eyes

It is good to exchange lighthearted words
And it would be great to share in a joke.

I am a human
who wrestles with
the separation
sickness of the ego and
hungers for liberation.

Think of the succeeding pages layered
One over another as the days of
Winter and the white of paper is like
A succession of snowy days wherein

The snow isn't soiled and the scenery
Is pristine and the weight of the cold burns
The skin and yet allows for the comfort
Of wearing warm clothes balanced by quiet

In which the sound of cars resonates in
The air differently from summer noise
Which is a numbing concatenation —
And doesn't the winter cast a spell and

Isn't it odd to gaze at the frozen
Yet wild gesticulation of bare trees?

Crows and cardinals
squirrels grasping ahold of
the creases of the
bark of the barren trees bring
a prominence to the trees.

A desk a window and snow on the hedge
Just a couple of feet outside are a
Point of departure and the glowing clouds
Swallow distance and yet there is freedom

To balance my sense of myself wherein
Time flows behind me like the frothy wake
Of a ship and if I choose what happened
Yesterday can be a weight on my mind

And if I'm energized and nimble this
Moment imposes itself quietly
And eyes that see are the apertures through
Which the cosmos is gazing at itself

And I know that even when I'm angry
Or afraid it is fitting to be here now.

Quiet emptiness
undergirds hubbub
concatenation
and I hold in my being
a return ticket to now.

I do like saying hippopotamus
Because it is a buoyant happy sound
The first two syllables kind of tiptoe
The last three stampede pell-mell together

Hip-po-potamus

Just saying the word lightens my spirit
And for fun I pop every single p

Hi**pp**o**p**otamus

I say it with a rising inflection

Hippo*potamus*

And then with a sinking inflection

*Hippo*potamus

It goes with a maniacal creature
A dopey jowly roly-poly brute
A rather irascible animal
With a small tail and ears — and a huge mouth

When I have my next opportunity
I do intend to say it happily.

The problem is in
casual conversation
I don't remember
ever having had the chance
to say hi**p**-**p**o-*potamus*.

Monkey Mind

You must not think about monkeys this week
Said the guru to his disciple and
The disciple thought "how easy as I
So seldom think about monkeys" but while

Walking home baboons came to mind and when
Meditating chimpanzees bothered him
And gorillas disturbed his dreams and at
Breakfast mountain monkeys with red bottoms

Troubled him and so it went for a week
And the disciple became angry and
Said to the guru "You told me not to
Think about monkeys knowing that saying

So would make me obsessed with monkeys" and
The guru smiled and said "Now you understand."

I have resolved as
a Minnesotan who does
remove the snow from
driveways that I simply won't
think about snow this winter.

I shoveled the light snow from the driveways in
In the dark of New Year's Eve because the
Forecasted temps were for brutal cold which
I wanted to avoid — I finished off the

Year watching a video and went to
Bed an hour before midnight — inside
My dreams there were lynxes and cheetahs and
Cougars and each of the cats ran in its

Own style — before waking I saw robots
Dancing in the air — I awoke refreshed
To hear Kitcat galloping through the house
Which he does apart from predatory

Impulse but with sudden bursts of nonsense
And an abundance of enthusiasm.

The morning sky of
New Year's Day is clear of
clouds — all sorts of
birds are darting between the
trees — fresh snow is very bright.

I am bored and browse the Internet seeing
A site of Old West photos that displays
The Dalton Gang shot dead and laid on boards
After they had failed to rob the bank in

1892 Coffeyville Kansas
And there are Buffalo Bill and Wild Bill
Hickok and then I observe a youthful
Face without whiskers and I notice her

Beautiful hair and womanly form clothed
In cowboy gear with hat and boots and
She holds a Henry repeating rifle —
Her face and relaxed shoulders express a

Confidence at home on the frontier and
Oh! how easily I could have loved her.

She robbed stagecoaches
was captured and imprisoned
for several years
in the 1890s the
caption barely explains.

A photograph from 1863
Shows samurai Koboto Santaro
Wearing a blue vest and plated armor —
The caption says that this type of armor

Appeared in fourth century Korea
Or China — it looks sophisticated
And lightweight — the helmet is festooned with
Gold wings and a disk which could be either

The sun or moon — his face is protected
By a hardened mask exaggerated
With the brutal features of a demon
And only a small portion of skin is

Visible about his eyes — he handles
A large white ceremonial tassel.

The two katana slung
within easy grasp of
the samurai bespeak
a keen lethality.

A recording of my beatnik guru
Alan Watts leads me to think that I've grasped
The point while I am pedaling hard on
My stationary bike in my living

Room as he simply says that it is a
Metaphysical truth that every thing
Has an inside and an outside and yet
The boundary between them isn't real

And happenings can't be separated
Into isolated events and when
One sees into the truth of the nature
Of things then the squirming of the frightened

Ego is unnecessary because
It's no more substantial than a bubble.

The problem is I
can't stop feeling that I'm
somebody going
somewhere progressing even
on a stationary bike.

The predicament comes at 3 a.m.
When I awake and can't return to sleep
And if I could return to sleep that would
Be a skillful trick of liberation —

I am tense from thinking about what
Happened yesterday and also about
What could happen tomorrow — I know such
Thinking is futile and yet my body

Turns and my mind is busy — trying to
Relax isn't relaxing — the more I
Try the more enmeshed I am — energy
Simmers but my thoughts lack the potency

Of spontaneous choice and as I yearn
For sleep I watch my mind work uselessly.

I cannot do what
I'd like to do but can't stop
trying to do it
as I don't yet know how to
make effortless effort.

I drove to a clinic in White Bear Lake
To get the booster shot of the vaccine
For COVID-19 as the numbers of
Cases of the latest variant of

The virus are exploding not only
In America but around the world
While it's a good sign that this version is
Much more infectious but also much less

Deadly signaling perhaps that every
Person will get it eventually
But it will be no more dangerous than
A cold so that we can throw away our

Masks and the bureaucrats can stop forcing
People to take vaccines that aren't working.

Closing businesses
demanding the wearing of
ineffective masks
were measures driven by fear
as the virus virused.

Alan Watts describes the trick of letting
Go of an arrow without conscious thought
As the best archers do aim and release
Spontaneously without a tangle

Of thought — if one aims and afterward
Decides to let go a complication
Arises — one has to decide when to
Decide — which becomes a predicament —

I aim for liberation but might be
Happy with relaxation — I seek love
But may be satisfied with companions —
I loiter over a keyboard at a

Window waiting for ethereal words
But I'll type this ordinary poem.

The shadows of trees
have lengthened on the snow on
the ground and on the
roofs of homes until the sun
sinks and all the shadows merge.

Sun sinks
Shadows of trees on snow merge —
crow is on a branch.

—*Tekkan*

www.ingramcontent.com/pod-product-compliance
Lightning Source LLC
Chambersburg PA
CBHW040421100526
44589CB00021B/2787